More of
THE WORLD'S GREATEST
PRAISE SONGS
50 Favorite Songs of Worship

Shawnee Press, Inc. §
A Subsidiary of **Music Sales Corporation**
1221 17th Avenue South • Nashville, TN 37212

Visit Shawnee Press online at www.shawneepress.com/songbooks

How Great Is Our God

Words and Music by
CHRIS TOMLIN, JESSE REEVES and ED CASH

Holy Is the Lord

Words and Music by
CHRIS TOMLIN and LOUIE GIGLIO

Awesome Is the Lord Most High

Words and Music by
CHRIS TOMLIN, JESSE REEVES,
CARY PIERCE and JON ABEL

praise You to - geth - er, for now and— for - ev - er. How

awe - some— is the Lord Most— High.— Raise your

Hal - le - lu - jah, hal - le - lu -

- jah.

Blessed Be Your Name

Words and Music by
BETH REDMAN and MATT REDMAN

Fast four, with energy ♩ = 116 - 120

1. Bless - ed be___ Your name___ in the land that___ is plen-
2. Bless - ed be___ Your name___ when I'm found in___ the des-
3. Bless - ed be___ Your name___ when the sun's shin - ing down
4. Bless - ed be___ Your name___ on the road marked___ with suf-

_ ti - ful,___ where Your streams of___ a - bun - dance flow,___ bless - ed
_ ert place,___ tho' I walk thru the wil - der - ness,___ bless - ed
___ on me, when the world's "all as it___ should be," bless - ed
_ fer - ing, tho' there's pain in the of - fer - ing, bless - ed___

1, 3.
2, 4.

___ be Your name.___
___ be Your name.___
___ be Your name.___
___ be Your name.___

Beautiful One

Words and Music by
TIM HUGHES

Lord, Reign in Me

Words and Music by
BRENTON BROWN

Steady four ♩ = 94 - 100

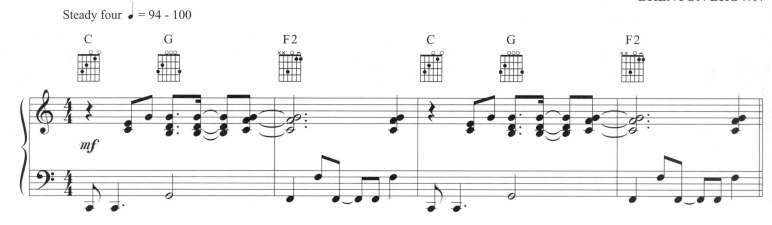

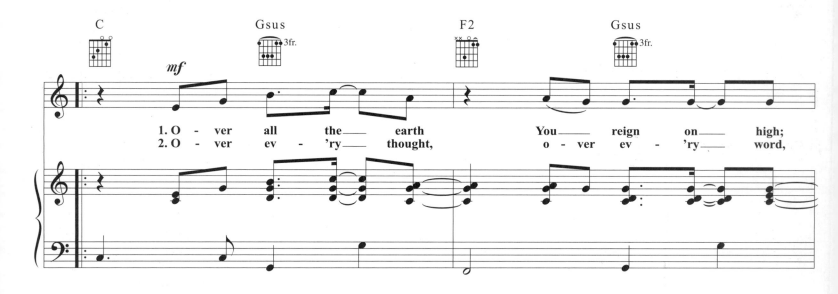

1. O - ver all the___ earth You___ reign on___ high;
2. O - ver ev - 'ry___ thought, o - ver ev - 'ry___ word,

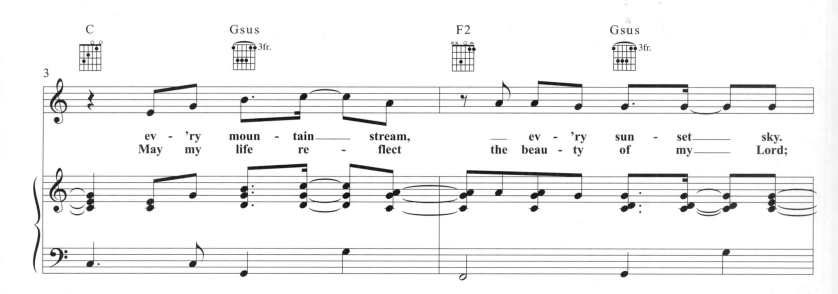

ev - 'ry moun - tain___ stream, ___ ev - 'ry sun - set___ sky.
May my life re - flect the beau - ty of my___ Lord;

so won't You reign in me a - gain.

Lord, reign in___ me, reign in Your___ pow'r, o - ver all my___ dreams,

in my dark - est hour. You are the Lord of all I am,___

The Wonderful Cross

Words and Music by
JESSE REEVES, CHRIS TOMLIN and J. D. WALT

With feeling ♩ = 90 - 94

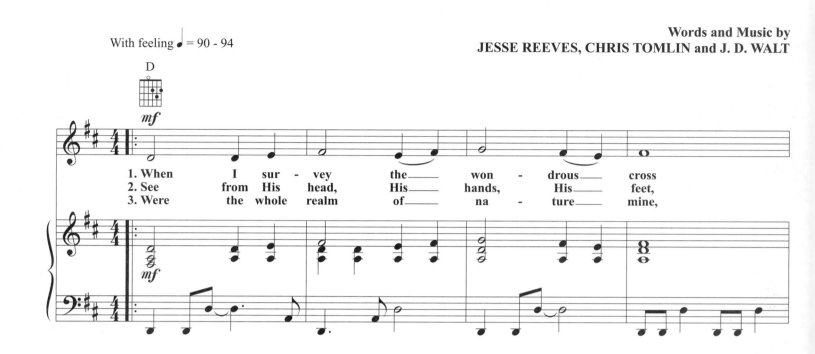

1. When I sur - vey the won - drous cross
2. See from His head, His hands, His feet,
3. Were the whole realm of na - ture mine,

on which the Prince of glo - ry died,
sor - row and love flow min - gled down;
that were an of - f'ring far too small:

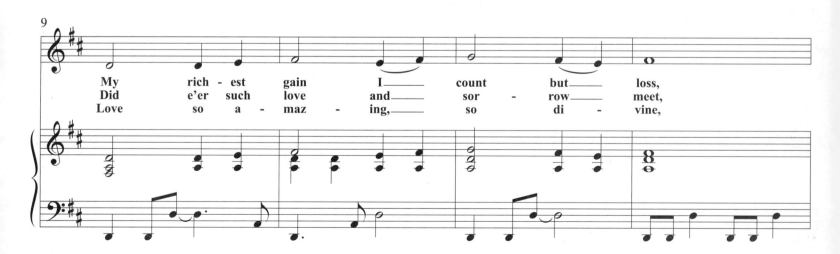

My rich - est gain I count but loss,
Did e'er such love and sor - row meet,
Love so a - maz - ing, so di - vine,

El Shaddai

Words and Music by
MICHAEL CARD and JOHN THOMPSON

Indescribable

Words and Music by LAURA STORY
Additional Lyrics by JESSE REEVES

Enough

Words and Music by
CHRIS TOMLIN and **LOUIE GIGLIO**

That's Why We Praise Him

**Words and Music by
TOMMY WALKER**

It Is You

Words and Music by
PETER FURLER

Medium groove ♩ = 76 - 80

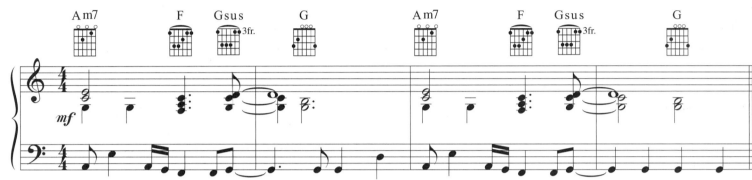

As we lift up our hands___ will You meet us here?

___ As we call on Your name___ will You meet us here?___

Your Grace Is Enough

Words and Music by
MATT MAHER and CHRIS TOMLIN

The Happy Song

**Words and Music by
MARTIN SMITH**

He Reigns

Words and Music by
PETER FURLER
and STEVE TAYLOR

With joy and energy ♩ = 96 - 100

Last time to Coda

Be the Centre

Words and Music by
MICHAEL FRYE

With a groove ♩°= 90 - 100

Every Move I Make

Words and Music by
DAVID RUIS

La, la, la, la, la, la, la. La, la, la, la, la, la, la.

Grace Like Rain

Words and Music by
CHRIS COLLINS and TODD AGNEW

but now I see so clear - ly.
I first be - lieved.
we'd first be - gun.

Hal - le - lu - jah, grace like rain falls down on me;

Hal - le - lu - jah, all my stains are washed a - way,

Last time to Coda

they're washed a - way.

2. 'Twas grace

they're washed a - way, yeah.

they're washed a - way. Hal - le - lu - jah, yeah.

3. When

Let My Words Be Few

Words and Music by
MATT REDMAN and **BETH REDMAN**

Let Everything That Has Breath

Words and Music by
MATT REDMAN

He Knows My Name

Words and Music by
TOMMY WALKER

Lord, Let Your Glory Fall

Words and Music by
MATT REDMAN

The Noise We Make

With energy and joy ♩ = 126 - 130

Words and Music by
JESSE REEVES and CHRIS TOMLIN

Famous One

Words and Music by
CHRIS TOMLIN and JESSE REEVES

Upbeat and flowing ♩. = 65 - 68

You _____ are the Lord, _____ the fa - mous One,

fa - mous One. Great _____ is Your name in all _____

Sing to the King

Words and Music by
BILLY JAMES FOOTE
and CHARLES SILVESTER HORNE, 1910

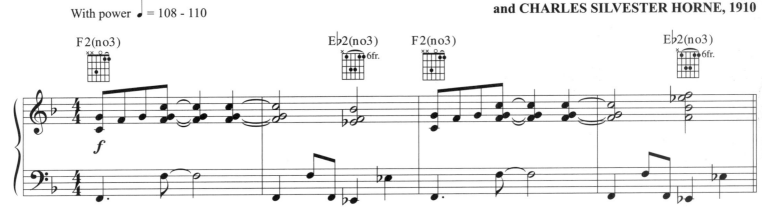

1. Sing to the King who is com - ing to reign,
2. For His re - turn - ing is we watch and we pray,

glo - ry to Je - sus, the
we will be read - y the

Refiner's Fire

(Purify My Heart)

Words and Music by
BRIAN DOERKSEN

Read - y to do Your will.

Read - y to do Your will.

Once Again

Words and Music by
MATT REDMAN

Salvation

Words and Music by
CHARLIE HALL

E5
6fr.

Let all the prod - i - gals___ run home;___ ___ All of cre - a - tion waits___ and groans. Lord, we've heard of Your___ great fame; Fa - ther, cause all to shout___ Your name.

(Fermata last time) *Fine*

NC

Let God Arise

Words and Music by
CHRIS TOMLIN

Not to Us

Words and Music by
JESSE REEVES and CHRIS TOMLIN

Take My Life
(Holiness)

Words and Music by
SCOTT UNDERWOOD

Give Us Clean Hands

Words and Music by
CHARLIE HALL

The Power of Your Love

Words and Music by
GEOFF BULLOCK

This Kingdom

Words and Music by
GEOFF BULLOCK

We Want to See Jesus Lifted High

Words and Music by
DOUG HORLEY

Fast, driving four ♩ = 124 - 132

We want to see Je - sus lift - ed high,_____ a ban-ner that flies_____ a - cross_____ this land,_____ That all men might see_____ the truth_____ and know_____

step we're mov - ing for - ward, lit - tle by lit - tle tak - ing ground.

Ev - 'ry prayer a pow - er - ful weap - on, strong - holds

come tum - bl - ing down, _____ and down, _____ and down, _____ and down. _____

D.S. al Fine
(to meas. 5)

Hungry
(Falling on My Knees)

Words and Music by
KATHRYN SCOTT

With a groove ♩ = 86 - 90

1. Hun-gry, I come to You, for I know You sat-is-fy.
2. Bro-ken, I run to You, for Your arms are o-pen wide;

I am emp-ty, but I know Your love
I am wear-y, but I know Your touch

Let It Rise

Words and Music by
HOLLAND DAVIS

1. Let the glo - ry of the Lord rise a - mong us, let the
(2. Let the) songs of the Lord rise a - mong us, let the

glo - ry of the Lord rise a - mong us; Let the
songs of the Lord rise a - mong us; Let the

prais - es of the King rise a - mong us, let it rise.
joy of the King rise a - mong us, let it rise.

O Praise Him
(All This for a King)

Words and Music by
DAVID CROWDER

1. Turn your ear to heav-en, and hear the noise in-side, the sound of an-gel's awe, the sound of an-
2. Turn your gaze to heav-en, and raise a joy-ous noise. The sound of sal-va-tion come, the sound of res-

You Are Holy
(Prince of Peace)

Words and Music by
MARC IMBODEN and TAMMI RHOTON

Jesus, Lover of My Soul

Words and Music by
PAUL OAKLEY

D.S. al Fine
(to meas. 2)

his - to - ry____ it - self____ be - longs____ to You.____

Al - pha and____ O - meg - a, You have

loved_____ me,____ and I will share____ e - ter -

ni - ty with_____ You.____ It's all a - bout

Big House

Words and Music by
**MARK STUART, BARRY BLAIR,
BOB HERMAN and WILL McGINNISS**

I don't know if you got a yard___ with a ham-mock in the shade.

2. I don't know if you got some shel - ter, say, a place___ to hide.
3. All I know, it's a big ol' house___ with rooms for ev - 'ry - one.

I don't know if you live with friends___ in whom you can___ con - fide.
All I know, is___ lots of land,___ where we can play___ and run.

Stomp

Words and Music by
KIRK FRANKLIN, GEORGE CLINTON, Jr.,
GARRY M. SHIDER, and WALTER MORRISON

Late - ly, I've been go - in' thru some things that's real - ly got me down. ___

I need some - one, some - bod - y to help me come and turn my life a -

I Can Only Imagine

Words and Music by
BART MILLARD

Shout to the North

Words and Music by
MARTIN SMITH

Surrender

Words and Music by
MARC JAMES

Strong four, not too slow ♩ = 66 - 72

1. I'm giv-ing You— my heart,— and all that is— with-in.
2. I'm sing-ing You this song,— I'm wait-ing at— the cross.

— I lay it all— down— for the sake of You,— my King.
And all the world— holds dear,— — I count it all— as loss

How Deep the Father's Love For Us

Words and Music by
STUART TOWNEND

In the Secret

Words and Music by
ANDY PARK

No Sacrifice

Words and Music by
JASON UPTON

Lifesong

With Joy! ♩ = 110 - 116

Words and Music by
MARK HALL

1. Emp - ty hands held___

(2.)___ high,   life,

such small   sac - ri -

a liv - ing___ sac - ri -

Thank You

**Words and Music by
RAY BOLTZ**

each life___ some-how touched . by your gen - er - os - i - ty.
but I am al - most sure there were tears___ in___ your eyes.

___ Lit - tle things that you___ had done,___ sac - ri - fic - es made,
As Je - sus took your hand,___ ___ and you stood be - fore___ the Lord,

un - not - iced on the___ earth,___ in heav - en now pro -
He said, "My child, look a - round you, for great is now your re -

1.
claimed.

2.
ward.

EXCITING NEW SONGBOOKS
from SHAWNEE PRESS

The World's Greatest Praise Songs
50 Favorite Songs of Worship

Titles include: **Here I Am to Worship · Come, Now Is the Time to Worship · Lord, I Lift Your Name on High · The Heart of Worship · Shout to the Lord ·** and more!

SB1003   Piano/Vocal/Guitar Collection $17.95

The Library of Contemporary Christian Music
240 pages, comb-bound book

Titles include: **Dare You to Move · Lifesong · Held · Dive · How Great Is Our God · Holy Is the Lord · I Can Only Imagine · Jesus Freak · Stomp · Thank You ·** and more!

SB1024   Piano/Vocal/Guitar Collection (comb bound) $24.95

iPrint - Praise & Worship
20 Favorite Songs of Praise/Over 100 pages of music on a CD ROM!
Print what you want…when you want it!

Titles Include: **How Great Is Our God · The Stand · Mighty to Save · Here I Am to Worship · Let Creation Sing · Holy Is the Lord ·** and more!

IPR6001   Piano/Vocal/Guitar Collection *plus* Chord Charts!...$16.95

iPrint - Piano
20 Best-Selling Arrangements/Over 70 pages of music on a CD ROM!
Print what you want…when you want it!

Arrangements from: Joseph M. Martin · Mark Hayes · Kurt Kaiser · Don Wyrtzen · and more!

IPR6002   Piano Collection $14.95

Jazzed on Hymns
Light Jazz Piano Arrangements of Favorite Hymns
Has CD with play-along tracks and printable chord charts!

Titles include: **Joyful, Joyful, We Adore Thee · Swing Low, Sweet Chariot · Amazing Grace ·** and more!

SB1016   Piano Collection $22.95

Jazzed on Christmas
Light Jazz Piano Arrangements of Favorite Carols
Has CD with play-along tracks and printable chord charts!

Titles include: **Joy to the World · Silent Night, Holy Night · Go, Tell It on the Mountain ·** and more!

SB1027   Piano Collection $22.95

For more information visit www.shawneepress.com/songbooks